From Stressing to Successing

Escape the Workweek Trap and Build a Life You Don't Need a Vacation From

Theresa Jenkins

This book is a work of nonfiction based on the author's personal experiences, opinions, and research. Every effort has been made to ensure accuracy at the time of publication. The advice and stories shared are not intended to replace professional guidance. Reader discretion is advised when applying any of the strategies mentioned.

Printed in the United States of America

First edition, 2025

DEDICATION

To the women who showed up with open minds, honest feedback, and full plates at my publishing party—thank you for helping me polish these pages into something real, something powerful, and something worth sharing. Your input gave this book the clarity and confidence it needed.

To my husband—my biggest encourager, my sounding board, and the calm to my chaos. Thank you for giving me the space to dream, the support to pursue those dreams, and the love that makes it all feel worth it.

This book is for anyone who knows they were meant for more—but needed a reminder that they're allowed to go get it.

Table of Contents

INTRODUCTION

From Stressing to Success(ing)

Monday through Friday, you have an alarm set before sunrise. You struggle to wake up, snoozing your alarm a time or two—or 12 times if you are a psychopath. I wouldn't call anyone a psychopath directly, but if you share a living space with someone you love, learn to wake the hell up on one alarm.

Back to my illustration: you have to be in traffic on your commute to work. Everyone is "in a rush." Nobody wants to let the next driver into their lane out of fear that they'll reach their destination a millisecond later. Maybe you have a five-minute commute because you have the luxury of living where you work—or working where you live. Or perhaps you're part of the majority that lives outside the city and commutes in, spending 30, 45, or even 60 minutes in traffic, which may or may not feel like hell depending on whether you've invested in an express lane pass.

Then, you work 8, 10, or 12 hours, living by other people's rules. Work tells you when you can and can't take a vacation, how to do the job that you're still paying off debt to learn in the first place. You have quotas. You can't be late. You get an occurrence if "life happens" and your cat eats the dog's food, and now it's sick. Or some not-so-intelligent person causes an traffic accident due to their lack of attention and awareness, and now your GPS of the highway looks like ketchup and mustard. Or perhaps you're sick because you work around other humans who have never taken a damn class on hand hygiene.

All in all, it feels shitty to live by anybody else's rules but your own. People create rules from their minds that make sense to them and occasionally benefit everyone else involved. Every job needs to have a grace period without assuming people want to abuse it.

Oh, and after a day of listening to other people's shit at work—whether they love or hate their job, their life, or whatever else—they send you right back into traffic. Only this time, it's worse because more of the world is awake, including the millionaire YouTubers, rich heirs, stay-at-home parents—blah, blah, blah.

Writing those nearly 400 words just stressed me the fireball out. Yes, I said fireball.

Assuming I publish this book (which I will), I'd like it to be available in all markets, so I have to watch my mouth. Lol. Plus, fireball sounds cool.

Like many, many, many other Americans, I dealt with this typical, everyday stress. Can you believe that's the norm—at least in America? EVERY. SINGLE. DAY.

Americans are out here running on expensive coffee our assets prove we can't afford, constantly exposed to a debilitating amount of decibels. Everyone has a common goal: to provide for themselves and/or their family and to have enough money to retire when (or if) they want to.

Well, lifelong stress is not the answer. Allow me to tell you how, at shy of 30 years young, I've created a life where I have at least 20 days off per month instead of working the traditional 20 days per month.

My life went from stressing to successing. (Yes, I'm making up words and phrases in this book, but I'm the author. Aren't you interested in getting into my head to see how the heck I cracked the code?)

Money is great. I love me some money. However, do not for one second believe you need a lot of it to get to the place I'm about to take you.

I'm writing this book with $60 left in my personal spending money for the next seven days. But that's by choice, not by fate. As I've found satisfaction, joy, and fulfillment within myself—through a series of intentional choices—I've realized I need less shit. Sorry. I need fewer things.

I'm not brainlessly walking into Target, buying stuff I don't need. I'm not buying new clothes just because I can, when there are plenty of outfits in my closet that haven't touched my body in months. I'm not spending hundreds per month on "upkeep."

I am gorgeous. There are many people who would agree with my biased statement. I don't need to spend hundreds altering the masterpiece that God made.

CHAPTER 1

Can We Acknowledge That NORMAL is a SCAM?

When I Googled the meaning of "retire", a few definitions popped up. The most annoying one?

"Upon reaching the normal age for leaving employment"

I wanted to scream at my computer. "Normal age?"

That feels discretionary at best and ageist at worst. Maybe I'm being dramatic, but Google, your friends, and society are in no position to tell you when it's the "right time" to cease employment or leave a job.

Leave when you want to leave. Next chapter. Ha! I crack myself up.

But for real, the second definition made more sense:

"To withdraw to or from a particular place"

Now that I can get behind.

This whole idea that we should work the better part of our lives just to get a little cookie party at retirement and a measly $2,000 per month (or 1,589.80 British pounds, which—side note—I love saying pounds instead of "dollars", and no, I'm not British. At least not yet. Maybe I'll go live there one day).

Anyway, $2,000 a month?! What if that's not enough for the standard of living by then? What if I don't even make it to retirement?

I have no aspiration to wait until I'm half-alive to retire.

Imagine waiting to cease employment until one is 65, just to die by 77.

By the way, I Googled this too. Nearly three million search results say the average life expectancy is 77.5 years. Honestly, they should've just rounded it up to a solid 78 or down to a dramatic 77.

I don't want to die in the middle of summer. At least let me enjoy some spring and summer before I go. Take me out in the winter, when it's cold and nobody wants to leave their house anyway. Then I'll hop into my cozy little coffin.

(Do I keep that sentence? Feels kind of morgue-ish, but also very real. We'll see.)

Somewhere Along the Way, We Started Believing Stress = Success

You'll hear people say:

> "Work harder."
> "Push through."
> "Grind now, rest later."

There's this popular myth that you have to work harder to accomplish everything.

Why?

Who the fireball said that?

What if we worked well?
What if we worked efficiently?
What if we worked enthusiastically?
What if we worked REFRESHED?

Working hard does not always equal success. Working hard equals burnout.

Your Life is Like a GPS—Choose Your Route Wisely

Ever put a destination into Google Maps or Apple Maps and see multiple ways to get there?

Usually, you get three choices:

1. The Fastest Route – High-speed highways, high-stress traffic, cops waiting to give you a ticket, road rage everywhere.
2. The "Efficient" Route – A mix of highways and back roads, but still some chaos.
3. The "Scenic" Route – More stop lights, more turns, but peaceful AF.

You get to choose your path. And so does everyone else. So stop worrying about the path other people take and start focusing on your own damn route.

Let's Do an Activity (Yes, You Have Homework)

Grab a pen, open a notes app, or use your forehead—I don't care.

Step 1: Set a timer for 5–10 minutes.
Step 2: Write down everything you do in your life just because "society" told you to.
Step 3: Look at your list and question every single thing on it.

Because society isn't questioning YOU before it dumps all these expectations on your life.

Now, cross off or erase everything that doesn't fulfill you.

Let Me Go First... Here's What I Changed

Two years ago, my lightbulb moment happened. I snapped out of it and started cutting out the nonsense.

Here's what society says vs. what I actually think:

What Society Says	What I Say
"Work full-time."	Why? I don't even want to work part-time. Why am I **overcommitting** myself?
"Your coworkers are like family."	My **actual** family is my family. I love them more. I'd rather spend my time with them.
"You need a credit card for emergencies."	First credit card came out in the **1950s**. Did no one have "emergencies" before then?

"Put everything on a credit card for points."	I don't need a reward for spending **my own money.** I'm not in kindergarten.
"The American Dream = marriage + kids."	What if someone doesn't want either? Is there no "dream" for them?

My Reality Now?

I work when I want—literally 5–7 days per month.
I get 20+ days off per month (while most work 20 days ON).
I spend more time with my handsome husband than I do with coworkers.
I haven't used a credit card in over a year.
My $1000 starter emergency fund replaces the need for a piece of plastic.

By the way, in one whole year, I haven't even had a $300 emergency—so $1000 has been doing me just fine.

Success: My Definition vs. My Husband's

On a long-ass car ride home, my husband and I got into a conversation—one of those deep, thought-provoking, why-am-I-even-thinking-this-hard-on-a-Saturday kind of talks. He was, as usual, bragging about me to his classmates, talking about my success, my career moves, and how I'm basically out here making boss moves like it's second nature.

I listened, I laughed, I smiled… and then curiosity got the best of me.

"What about my path do you actually recognize as successful?" I asked.

I wanted to know—out of all the adults he knows, from elders to friends to colleagues, why am I the one he constantly brags about? What sets me apart in his eyes?

His answer caught me off guard. He told me that, to him, success in a career means being able to walk into any situation and get what you want out of it. The fact that I can pick up and get a job anywhere without stress, negotiate my way into higher pay, better schedules, and more freedom, and never have to feel stuck or desperate in a job—that, to him, is success.

And while I absolutely love this observation (because, let's be real, that is a flex), it's not my personal definition of success. His perspective made me realize something major—success looks different for everybody. What one person finds impressive, another person might not even think twice about.

For me, success is control over my time.
Success is being able to work minimal days per month and still thrive.
Success is having hobbies and actually having the time to enjoy them—and even monetize them.
Success is being able to volunteer at events because I genuinely want to, not because I'm chasing a paycheck.
Success is knowing that if I were fired today, all it would take is one phone call, and I'd be hired somewhere else before the ink even dried on my termination letter.

I have built something that will always be a backup plan, and I'm building even more to make sure my family's income and lifestyle are never at the mercy of an employer, an economy, or a "what if."

Meanwhile, my husband—who has a bachelor's degree, years of work experience, and insane talent—has struggled with finding a job in a new industry. We're talking hundreds of applications, barely any callbacks, and no offers. He's watching me collect job opportunities like gumballs from a 10-cent machine with a whole dollar, while he's out here with the same dollar but no gumballs in sight.

That's when I realized—I may feel successful because I have what most believe to be job security, an illusion in itself, and time freedom, a true asset. But his idea of success is being able to find work he loves just as easily as I do.. That conversation made me reevaluate how I can better support his career goals the same way he supports mine.

Job security is an illusion. It's not real. Travel contracts can get canceled. For 2025, an estimated 222,000 job cuts have been announced. One company I work with has even started requiring employees to go home early if work is slow, and going as far as to call them while at home to tell them not to come in due to low productivity. So, what is job security, really?

So, here's a challenge for you:

1. Ask two people you know how they define success. Notice the commonalities and differences between their answers.
2. Define success for yourself. What does it look like? What does it feel like?
3. If you're married or in a relationship, think about how you can help support your partner in feeling successful, too.

Because at the end of the day, you can't chase someone else's version of success—you have to define your own.

What is Success, Really?

Let's chat. Success is not:

A number in your bank account.
A promotion at work.
An award printed off Canva with your name on it.

Success is a FEELING.

✓ Success is waking up happy with your life.
✓ Success is looking in the mirror and smiling back at yourself.
✓ Success is people wanting to be around you because of how you make them feel.

NORMAL IS A SCAM. STRESS DOES NOT EQUAL SUCCESS.

Now, let's go build a life that actually feels like yours.

CHAPTER 2

Why Do People Wear Stress Like It's Some Badge of Honor?

You are not a hero.

I think being "busy" has become a primary personality characteristic for way too many people. Nothing excites me more than looking at my Apple Calendar and not seeing that tiny gray dot under every single day of the month. If you have an iPhone—or know someone with an iPhone—I challenge you to look at the monthly view of their calendar. Are there more dots than blank days?

If you still use a paper calendar, this is the equivalent of writing an obligation under every single day.

Being "busy" all the time is lame.

How many times have you heard someone proudly say:

> "I work through lunch."
> "I stayed late at work again."
> "I'll sleep when I'm dead."

Sorry, I'm not working hungry. And I'm especially not working hard while hungry.

You are going to get my most mediocre work when all I can think about is an egg white omelet with extra jalapeños.

Over the years, I've come across people who do the bare minimum, and society calls them lazy.

I disagree.

I see people who:

> Show up at the time they're scheduled.
> Do the job they were trained to do.
> Use downtime to rest, reset, or enjoy life.

And yet, the overworked, stressed-out folks judge them.

> "They're lazy."
> "They don't care."
> "They should be doing more."

Or… maybe they just don't care about the things YOU care about.

Maybe they don't care about going above and beyond for a system that won't even remember their name when they leave.

Maybe they're simply minding their own damn business.

I want to spit-fire a series of questions at you:

> When was the last time you called an elder to check on them?

When was the last time you drank a full cup of coffee while it was still hot?
When was the last time you did something for yourself that actually felt good?
When was the last time you went a full week without setting an alarm?
When was the last time you were enjoying life so much that you forgot what day of the week it was?
When was the last time you took a vacation?
When was the last time you got 8 full hours of sleep?
When was the last time you made a home-cooked meal?
When was the last time you had a date night with your partner?
When was the last time you sat and listened to someone talk about their interests—even if you didn't care—just because you love them?
When was the last time you discussed your hopes and dreams?

I'll wait.

I'm sure you could use a moment of silence to process the fact that you've been so "busy" that you haven't even been living your life.

Life has been passing you by.

Being constantly exhausted, overstimulated, and unfulfilled does not make you smart, important, or valued. It just makes you burnt out. And burnout? That's just stress that's gone unmanaged.

I'm ready to help you change this.

Action Step: Audit Your Life Like a Boss

Let's get real. I want you to think about your daily routine—and I mean really think about it.

Write it down, type it out, or just go through it in your head. Walk yourself through a typical day (or two) in your week and consider every single factor.

To help you brainstorm:

> What time do you wake up?
> How do you start your day?
> What time are you getting in bed at night?
> Do you live alone or with others? What do interactions in your home look like?
> Do you pack your lunch, eat out, or skip meals entirely?
> How do you commute? Car? Train? Bus? Bike? Walk?
> Is your commute silent or filled with noise?
> Do you listen to music, podcasts, or YouTube? Who do you listen to?
> What does your meals look like?
> Are you physically active at all—besides walking from your car to your job?

Got your answers? Cool.

Now, I want you to delete at least three things from your daily routine that bring you zero joy and zero fulfillment.

Congratulations. You've just made time for what actually matters.

Now, go back to the list of questions I "spit-fired" at you earlier. Pick one or more that resonate with you, and prioritize adding it into your routine this week.

You should have time for it now that we've cut out some nonsense.

The Time I Let "Being Busy" Run My Life (And How I Snapped Out of It)

I remember back in 2021, I was working as a traveling sonographer on the West Coast while maintaining a PRN staff position in Atlanta, Georgia. Sounds harmless, right? Well…

I'd work 3×12-hour shifts or 4×10-hour shifts on the West Coast… then immediately fly across the country to work 1 or 2 more 12-hour shifts in Atlanta—just to keep a job I was scared to lose. Then I'd fly back to my travel contract.

Let's break this chaos down:

I was switching time zones monthly (Pacific to Eastern and back).
I was losing money on flights that cost more than the shifts I was working.
I was burning time, energy, and sanity for no real gain.
I was working 64 hours per week, (once per month) in a constant state of jet lag.
Those weeks, I was working 10 days straight with no break.

Why? Because I was afraid.

I loved my Atlanta job. I feared that if I stepped away—even temporarily—I'd lose the opportunity forever. I feared my travel contract would get canceled, and I'd be left jobless.

Reality check: This was all in my head.

At the time, we were still in the middle of COVID, and there were AT LEAST 300 travel ultrasound positions available at any given moment.

Even if one facility didn't need me, hundreds of others did—even if it meant my husband and I had to move to the middle of Alaska for three months.

It was never the end of the world.

But I was running myself (and my marriage) into the ground because society told me:

> "You can't leave a 'good job.'"
> "One day, travel healthcare will disappear."
> "You always need a backup plan."

Sound familiar?

Let me tell you what actually happened:

> That job I was afraid to lose? Welcomed me back with open arms when I was ready.
> That travel healthcare career people said would "go away"? It's still in full demand.
> That fear-based decision-making? Completely unnecessary.

I was so busy trying to hold onto something that wasn't even slipping away.

The Big Lesson: Stop Letting "What-Ifs" Run Your Life

I spent six months overworking, stressing, flying across the country, burning money, and wrecking my peace for NO REASON.

I wasted so much time doing things that didn't fulfill me—because I thought that if I didn't, some secret society of "success police" would show up in white Escalades, bag my head, throw me in the trunk, and arrest me for not following their norms.

It was ridiculous. I was busy as hell, but I still didn't feel like I accomplished anything. And now? In 2025, I'm writing this book.

That job I feared losing? Still there. That career I thought would disappear? Thriving. That need to be "busy" to feel important? Completely gone.

Final Thoughts: Stop Worshipping "Busy" and Start Prioritizing Fulfillment

The truth is simple:

On the other side of comfort is what you already know.
On the other side of risk could be the biggest blessing of your life.

If you're always busy, you're too distracted to recognize when something amazing is right in front of you.

Enjoy this life. You don't get to live this one again.

Cheers to ditching the addiction of being busy and actually living a life of fulfillment.

CHAPTER 3

Financial Freedom: (Do you have to sell your soul to achieve it?)

Moneeeeey Stress
Money stress honestly should be its own mental health condition that requires focused attention from a licensed clinician.

The way in which someone has to escape the scarcity mindset and break free from the paycheck-to-paycheck cycle in order to free themselves from money stress is wild. I too, struggle with this at times.

When I learned that doctors, lawyers, heirs, and even lottery winners were living paycheck to paycheck, I knew the rest of us were fireballed.

80% of Americans Are Broke. Let's Talk About It.

"Broke" in this context means living paycheck to paycheck—where a person's expenses outweigh their income or assets.

And guess what? That 80% includes:

- Low-income earners

- Middle class
- Six-figure earners
- Entrepreneurs
- Even people living on assistance

This 80% does not discriminate by race, ethnicity, political interest, state, education level—none of it.

So... why?

We live in America—the land of opportunity. We can leverage debt, make investments, and build wealth.

So why is 80% of the population still struggling?

The Real Reason Most People Are Broke

It comes down to a series of life choices.

> We buy things before we can afford them because "what if it's not there later?"
> We book vacations on "easy payment plans" without realizing how much it actually costs.
> We swipe our credit cards because we don't want to feel left out.
> We overspend to impress people who don't pay our bills.

Let's break this down.

Imagine you book a vacation that costs $3,600. Instead of paying upfront, you opt for a "simple" $100/month payment plan for 36 months. Seems doable, right?

Here's the gag:

The fine print says that if you miss just one payment, the interest skyrockets to 27%. Now, your $3,600 vacation just cost you $4,572. "But wait, that's not fair! It was just one day late!" Exactly.

We Are Drowning in "Appearances" Debt

We are broke because:

"I can't wear the same outfit twice on Instagram—people will think... (insert a completely delusional thought)."
"My cousin's sister's baby daddy's daughter's second birthday is in Madrid, Spain, and I HAVE to be there—even if I can't afford it."
"I make $1,500 a month, my bills are $2,800, I already have three trips planned this year... but YOLO!"

Dramatic? Maybe.

But so is the person who continuously lives outside of their means just because they're afraid of what people will think if—God forbid—they don't show up to an event empty-handed.

People are broke because no matter their income, they are financially illiterate. Financial illiteracy simply means lacking the knowledge to manage money. And I'll admit—it got me too. Two years ago, I was financially illiterate.

Breaking Free from Financial Illiteracy: Let's Fix This

SparkNotes version of how to deal with money:

Step 1: Calculate Your Real Monthly Expenses

Take all of your expenses over a 90-day period and divide by 3 to get your average monthly cost.

For example:

January: $3,000
February: $3,700
March: $2,300
Total: $9,000

$9,000 ÷ 3 = $3,000 per month.

So if your average monthly expenses are $3,000, you need to make sure you are bringing in at least $3,000 per month to maintain your current lifestyle.

Step 2: Stop Swiping Your Credit Card Like It's Monopoly Money

If you're swiping it without a plan, lock it away and hide the key.

Step 3: Pull a Free Credit Report & List Your Debts

You need to know what you owe before you can fix it.

Make an itemized list of every debt—big or small—including:

1. Credit cards
2. Car loans
3. Medical bills
4. Student loans
5. That sneaky "buy now, pay later" balance

Step 4: Start the Debt Snowball Method

Pay the minimums on ALL debts, but aggressively pay off the smallest one first. Use the following chart as an example.

See chart on next page.

Debt	Balance	Minimum Payment	Due Date
Credit Card #1	$70	$35	29th
Car Loan	$4,322	$250	13th
Credit Card #2	$5,766	$188	2nd
Student Loan #1	$11,784	$232	7th
Student Loan #2	$11,821	$76	12th

Pay the minimum on all debts every month. Once Credit Card #1 is paid off, roll that $35 minimum monthly payment into your next smallest debt payment. Now instead of paying $250/month for your car loan, you pay $285/month ($250 + $35)—paying it off faster. Repeat this process until all consumer debt is gone.

Step 5: Get Term Life Insurance

If you have anyone relying on your income, get a term life insurance policy—*period*. Term life insurance is coverage that lasts for a specific term, usually 10, 20, or 30 years. I personally recommend the 20- or 30-year option, especially if you're still building wealth or raising a family. It's affordable, straightforward, and gives your loved ones financial security if something unexpected happens.

Now, quick side note: there's a lot of buzz around whole life insurance, but here's the deal—whole life is expensive, complicated, and often sold as an investment when it's really not a great one for most people. You'll get more bang for your buck by choosing a high-value term policy and using the difference in cost to pay down debt, invest, or build your emergency fund. Keep it simple and protect your people.

And while we're here, I urge you to consider a policy for your children too. In my own family, we've experienced the unimaginable—two pediatric deaths under the age of ten. One child passed before their first birthday. My cousin was eight years old—healthy, happy, full of life, riding dirt bikes with a smile I still get chills remembering. One day he had a fever that spiraled into complications, and he never made it home. His final days were spent in a hospital—and that hospital wasn't free. Medical bills don't vanish just because someone passes away. Life insurance is about protecting your peace and your family's dignity during the hardest times. Get coverage for yourself, your spouse, and yes—even your children.

A good rule of thumb: Your annual income × 10.

Example: If you make $50,000 per year, get a $500,000 policy. This ensures your family isn't financially wrecked if something happens to you.

<u>Step 6: Build Your Emergency Fund</u>

Start with $1,000—this stops you from using credit cards for "emergencies."

Once you're debt-free, aim for 4-6 months of expenses saved up.

If your monthly expenses are $3,000, that means:
$12,000–$18,000 in a fully funded emergency fund.

Now that we've covered the basics...Let's talk about how to stop working for money. Because let's be real—you don't just want to "pay bills and die." You don't want to stress about money forever. You want to get to a place where your money works FOR you.

Action Step: Create your path to financial literacy

Grab a notebook or open a spreadsheet and go through Steps 1–6. Don't just read them—*do* them. Especially:

- List your real monthly expenses (use the 90-day average method).
- Pull your free credit report today (Experian, Equifax, or TransUnion).
- Make a debt list and highlight your smallest balance.
- Pick a day this week to price-check a term life insurance policy.
- Create a savings tracker to get that $1,000 emergency fund started.

If you do even half of this, you'll already be ahead of most people.

Let's Sacrifice Some Shii...

During my debt-free journey, I sacrificed a lot—or at least that's what other people called it. Personally, I just decided to be low maintenance for a while.

- I stopped getting my hair done once a month.
- I stopped paying for hair removal services and went back to shaving and tweezing.
- I stopped going to the nail salon every month.

- I made coffee at home instead of throwing $6 a day at Starbucks.
- I offered to do my husband's hair so he didn't have to spend extra money at the salon.
- I bathed my dog at home instead of paying the groomer.
- I planned our meals out instead of giving in to "we're tired" excuses every time we wanted to eat out.
- I practiced saying no to most invites that required me to swipe my debit card.
- I paused my gym membership for eight months and worked out at home or outside instead.

Let's break that down into real numbers:

Hair: $150 + tip
Husband's Hair: $100 + tip
Pedicure: $65 + tip
Wax: $100 + tip
Dinner for Two: $60
Brunch with Friends: $50
Dog Bath at Groomers: $32 + tip
Gym Membership: $30/month
Coffee: $6 each

If my husband and I both got our hair done at a salon, I got a pedicure and waxing, we went out for dinner twice, I went to brunch, I took my dog for his little fancy soap-and-water bath (with a bandana, of course—my dog owners, IYKYK), kept my gym membership, and had coffee twice a week, that would have added up to $630 per month.

$630 per month x 12 months = $7,560.

That's close to the downpayment amount I put down on my house.

None of these things are necessities. Anybody can sacrifice non-essentials for a year or two in order to better position their future.

I'm not saying never enjoy life—but I am saying find ways to enjoy life without needing your debit card to do it.

75 Days of No Excuses (And More Savings)

I also took on 75 Hard, a mental toughness challenge by Andy Frisella.

For 75 days straight, I:

1. Worked out twice a day
2. Drank one gallon of water per day
3. Read 10 pages of a nonfiction book per day
4. Stuck to a healthy meal plan I created
5. Didn't consume alcohol

Not only did I save a ton of money, but I also stopped making excuses for myself.

Get creative. Do what you gotta do.

How Sacrificing for One Year Changed My Entire Life

The sacrifices my husband and I made—along with other strategic moves—allowed us to pay off $42,000 of debt in just 12 months.

- Paid off all my student loans
- Paid off three cars
- Paid off two credit cards
- Paid off every medical bill that popped up

Debt was eating up **$1,845** of our **monthly** income.

To put that into perspective—there are people who don't even bring home $1,845 a month, and we were spending that much just on debt payments.

That's why I call this my testimony.

Reflection Prompt: Write down 3 "non-essentials" you can pause for 6–12 months to accelerate your debt-free journey. Think hair, nails, eating out, subscriptions, convenience shopping, etc. Circle the one that would free up the most cash without completely ruining your joy. Try pausing it for just 30 days and track the savings.

A Quick Note on Perspective

I know I've been speaking in first person for most of this book. I sprinkle in details about my marriage and how we tackled this together, but ultimately, this book is from my perspective—my strategies, my lessons, and my understanding of finances.

There will be a platform where I speak to married couples about what we did as a team… but that's a whole other book in itself.

Although I use "I" often, it's important to me that you understand why: I'm sharing what I've personally done, what actually worked, and what's worth considering in your own life. This isn't theory—it's lived experience. You get to take what resonates and leave what doesn't. But just know, I'd never recommend something I haven't done—or wouldn't do—myself.

How Cutting Expenses Allowed Me to Cut My Work Hours in Half

Because of those sacrifices, I now only need to work 5–7 days per month.

Instead of working 20+ days per month, I get 20+ days OFF.

I was able to cut my monthly expenses by 50%, which meant I had options:

1. Work less and still live comfortably.
2. Work the same amount but put extra money toward paying off more debt or going on more vacations.

I chose time over money.

I realized my time was way more valuable than maintaining my original income.

Now, I:

- Spend more time at home
- Have time to explore my passions and hobbies
- Cook more meals instead of relying on takeout
- Learn new skills instead of paying people to do everything for me

I realized how much I was capable of doing by myself, but I had been too tired, too rushed, and too drained to do it before.

How I Created a Passive Income Stream Without Spending a Dime

Because of my extra time, I finally had the chance to explore passive income.

And guess what? I didn't have to spend a single dime to start.

I wrote an e-book based on my own knowledge.

- I didn't pay a single cent to create or market it.
- I formatted it into a paperback for Amazon, which means Amazon now markets, prints, and handles customer service for me.
- I've already sold 40 copies at $4.99 each—without paid advertising.
- I create simple YouTube videos to help people discover me and my content.

I took something I already knew, put it into a sellable format, and let the internet do the work for me.

It Doesn't Take a Lot of Money or Time to Change Your Life

Where I am today didn't happen overnight. But it also didn't require extreme luck, a six-figure salary, or crazy risks. All it took was a little sacrifice. A lot of discipline. The confidence to believe I could take control of my finances.

And now?

I don't *need* a vacation—because I've built a life I don't want to escape from. But don't get it twisted, I still *want* vacations. I want to explore new places, meet new people, and unlock new parts of myself I didn't even know existed. There's a big difference between needing a break because you're overwhelmed and burned out, and simply wanting a new experience because your life already feels full and grounded. *Needing* a vacation usually signals something deeper—like stress, exhaustion, or imbalance. *Wanting* a vacation? That's curiosity, growth, and joy. It's a mindset shift.

End-of-Chapter Challenge:

Build Your Freedom Budget:

- Write down your current monthly income.
- Subtract your *true* monthly expenses (include all the things you *actually* spend money on).
- Then subtract all the "non-essentials" you could pause or cut for 3–6 months.
- Calculate how many fewer days you'd need to work per month with those savings.

Now ask yourself: *Would I rather continue working the way I do now… or create a life with more control over my days?* Your life won't change unless your habits do. Pick one financial change and implement it for the next 30 days. Track how it makes you feel, what changes, and what surprises you. Tiny shifts create massive momentum.

CHAPTER 4

My 2nd Favorite B-word, Boundaries

Are You Ready to Set Some Damn Boundaries?

Let me tell you something. There are a lot of people who are going to have offensive shit to say about you changing your life. If you do anything we discussed from Chapter 3, you're going to hear about it.

With the majority of people being broke, they don't know, like, or understand why you would sacrifice *now* to set yourself up for a better life *later*.

Your friends? They're gonna be upset.

> Oh, you don't want to do bottomless mimosas every weekend at an overpriced restaurant with so-so customer service?
> Oh, you don't want to go out to eat with three of us and just "split the bill evenly" even though our meals and drinks were triple the cost of your modest $30 entrée with free tap water?

When I tell you people are going to have shit to say, I am not kidding you.

However, you have to remember: they are living in a different mentality than you are.

You picked up this book because the idea of going from stressing to successing intrigued you. You are trying to escape the cycle that many people are trapped in.

Boundaries: The Fast Track to Success

I have to give credit to Rachel Hollis here. In her book *Girl, Stop Apologizing*, she wrote something that stuck with me: Every time you say yes to someone else, you're saying no to yourself. As if the title alone didn't already make me a fan, that one-liner sealed the deal.

It is very beneficial to limit the outside noise while making these huge shifts in your life.

Your parents, friends, and co-workers will still be there once you're done doing this important work within yourself. But if you keep letting them dictate your life, you'll never get to where you want to be.

The more focused you are on reaching that feeling of success, the faster you'll achieve it.

Think of it like a savings account. If you have a $1,000 savings goal and put $1 in every chance you get, it's going to take you 1,000 chances to reach your goal. If you put $100 in every chance you get, it's only going to take 10 chances to reach your goal.

Now, let me be clear: Success is **NOT** a monetary number. This example is just to put it into a perspective we can see and measure. Your success will likely look entirely different than what you ever imagined—hopefully even better. Because here's the thing about dreams and imagination: They can only extend as far as the information you have been exposed to.

If you never knew certain things were possible—especially possible for YOU—then how could you ever have dreamed of achieving them?

Success Requires Boundaries—Everywhere

I never planned to have 20+ days off per month. I simply planned to be financially free. Now, I don't know anyone working in corporate America that has the time freedom I have. I'm sure they exist, but I don't personally know them. I also don't know anyone my age who gets to enjoy life at the level I do. Hell, I don't even know anyone 50 and up that gets 20+ days off per month and still maintains their lifestyle. But here's the point: Most people don't even know this is an option. All we know is what jobs are available when we apply to them.

We don't know that boundaries, negotiations, and strategic decisions can create a completely different reality than the one society has trained us to expect.

And that's exactly what we're getting into next:

> How to set boundaries at work so you stop being overworked and under appreciated.
> How to negotiate better pay, better benefits, and better flexibility without fear.

How to set boundaries with family and friends so their opinions don't drain your progress.
How to set boundaries with yourself so you stop sabotaging your own success.

Because if you don't set the rules for your own life, someone else will set them for you.

Boundaries: What You Decide is Acceptable

Boundaries are defined as what you decide is acceptable in a situation or relationship. I feel it's necessary to define boundaries because so many people either don't know what they are, choose to ignore them, or choose not to make them at all. Since your life is your story, let's make this about you. What's some shii you've said yes to in the past thirty days that you shouldn't have? Now, think about how that worked out for you. I'll wait.

I find this chapter the slowest and hardest to write because, for me, boundaries are second nature. At the very least, I know what mine are. The hard part has always been implementing them—because I don't want to let others down. But I had to learn to let that shii go a while ago. You see, I LOVE my family. I LOVE myself. And I hate seeing outside influences disrupt that flow.

Boundaries at Work

So, my boss sent me a text. (Yes, I still have a boss—at least at the time of writing this book.) She asked me if I'd switch from my comfortable 12:00 PM – 8:30 PM shift to a loud, demanding, traffic-ball-busting 6:30

AM – 3:00 PM shift. I'm so happy that message sat in my inbox for an hour or so because I was enjoying some much-needed digital detox. Once I finally responded, my message read:

"No, thank you. Traffic during that shift is unfavorable for me."

Probably not the response she wanted to hear, but definitely the response I needed to send. I made sure not to overshare—because **BOUNDARIES**. However, once I got hold of my journal, I let my pen go off:

"Today, I said NO to a request to work earlier for five days where I would lose valuable time with my husband, be exposed to higher traffic volumes and higher Peach Pass rates. Plus, I would be setting a God-awful alarm for 4:45/5:00 AM AND losing $10 per day in shift differential. I said YES to me, my family, and my sanity—and NO to an opportunity that neither pleases me nor benefits me. Plus, that shift is busy, and the hard work you put in rarely comes with a thank you. So great job, Theresa!"

Honestly, being a work-in-progress people-pleaser, I am so proud of myself. A small part of me wanted to agree to help on one or two days, but WHY? WHY? There was clearly NO BENEFIT FOR ME! If you want to throw in some incentives, then we're talking. But favors? I stopped doing those. Because WHY? If I scratch your back, are you going to scratch mine? If I agree to disrupt my life to help my company for five days, and then I'm late one day, will I still be met with strife, an occurrence, or a write-up? Or will my five good deeds magically be there to protect me? Yeah… no. So, company favors? No, thank you. You do it.

It Is OK to Say No

I think work should be the first place you start setting up boundaries. Most employees do not get paid for their time outside of work. Therefore, your employer should have limited access to you and your time when you are not scheduled to produce for them. Let's not get it twisted, though—friends and family need boundaries too. Boundaries are walls of respect you put around yourself to protect yourself. Other people could and should do the same. I personally love how Beyoncé doesn't play about her family's peace and privacy. It's not up for debate, and it's not for sale. Good for her.

Boundaries with Family

The first thing that comes to mind? Stop letting other people tell you how to live your life. You have to earn a vote in the decisions that I make. Even then, I will open the polls when I'm taking votes. Until then, there is no absentee ballot for you to write in your opinions about my life. Shove your two cents where the sun doesn't shine.

I seek wisdom from those I trust, when I need it. But unsolicited advice? I've never received it and thought to myself, "Wow, I really wish I had listened to that verbal trespasser." However, I am an outgoing, self-sufficient young woman living in the year 2025. I can always find what I need when I need it.

Boundaries with Yourself

What do you want out of this life? When you look at yourself in the mirror, what do you see versus what do you want to see? How you see the world is largely shaped by how you see yourself. How you view yourself greatly impacts the decisions that you make.

Does the mirror reflect someone who feels stressed, overwhelmed, undervalued, overworked, unhappy? Is that where you want to be in life? Or are you wanting and/or needing a change? What would it take to get there? When considering the process of creating boundaries with yourself, think: discipline, structure, progress, and non-negotiables.

ACTION STEP: Define 3 Non-Negotiables

- Write down three boundaries you want to implement with yourself. These could include:
    - A screen-free hour before bed
    - Not working past 6 PM
    - Saying "no" to any invites that don't align with your goals

- Commit to practicing these boundaries for the next 7 days and document how they impact your peace and productivity.

75 Hard: My Journey to Self-Discipline

The Rules Outlined by Andy Frisella: Two 45-minute workouts. One must be outside (like actually outside, not just stepping outside your house... my husband had the nerve to suggest we could just walk inside a grocery store because it's "outside" our home. DUDE?!). I had to follow a nutritional plan of my choice. I had to drink one gallon of water (128 ounces—of straight-up water). No alcohol for 75 days. No wine, no liquor, no beer, not even kombucha (lol). One progress photo every day. Read 10 pages of a non-fiction book daily.

This challenge taught me boundaries—because if I was going to fully commit, then each requirement was a boundary in itself. I had to say no to things that didn't fit within these guidelines. Every single day, I had to look at myself in the mirror and decide: Was I going to break my word, my bond with myself? Or was I going to follow through? There were no excuses—just commitment.

The Power of Saying No to Protect Your Peace

At the end of this challenge—which I never actually viewed as "hard"—I came out a re-birthed version of me. I learned to say no to things that didn't align with my agenda. I learned the power of sleep so I could wake up and do it all again the next day. I learned to say no to happy hours and brunch invites. I learned to be comfortable being alone because I was on this journey for myself. And on Day 76? I was more confident. I made fewer excuses. I learned to prioritize myself.

The "Elusive" Story

One day at my long-term job, a coworker—someone I barely knew but had coexisted with for some time—casually called me "elusive."

All I heard was "loose", and for a second, I was deeply confused and mildly offended. Like, excuse me? I was literally standing there, minding my business, doing my job, and suddenly I'm being labeled as... loose? On the clock? The disrespect.

Of course, later that evening, curiosity got the best of me, and I did what any normal person does—I googled the word. Turns out, elusive means hard to find, unavailable on demand, difficult to track down, mysterious.

And suddenly, I had never been more proud in my life.

I wanted to go around telling people, "Yeah, I'm elusive. Can't catch me. Try again." Because honestly? It's a compliment.

I have gained a sense of confidence in my privacy. I share things on a need-to-know basis, and guess what? Most people don't need to know. Not everyone needs access to me, my schedule, or my life updates—not all the time, or even any of the time for that matter. I am not always available.

One day, I might be in Mazatlán learning to salsa, the next, I'm in Los Angeles eating street tacos, and a week later, I'm back in Atlanta visiting family. I do what feels right, when it feels right. And I love it that way.

Because here's the thing—when people always know what you're doing, they start feeling entitled to your time. They start feeling like they can disrupt it, insert themselves into it, or make demands on it. But when people know you value your time, they will respect it, too.

And let me tell you—people don't play games with me. They know I mean business. So come correct or don't come at all, O-K-A-Y?!

ACTION STEP: Audit Your Availability

- Take 24 hours and keep track of how many people reach out to you that day (text, call, DM, in person).

- Of those interactions, ask yourself: Which ones were necessary, and which ones were just people trying to access your time without purpose?
- Journal your observations. What boundaries can you set this week to reduce unnecessary access to your time?

Owning your time speaks volumes. It makes people take notice. It makes people respect you in ways you don't even have to ask for. Because let's be real—people envy those who have their time management down to a science.

Being elusive is a power move. It means you have boundaries. It means people don't call you for foolishness because they know better. It means you are not someone they can predict, control, or take for granted.

And let's be honest—there is nothing intriguing about a person whose every move you can predict. Where's the excitement in that?

So yeah, call me elusive. I'll take it as a compliment every single time.

ACTION STEP: Create a "Boundaries Blueprint"

Grab a sheet of paper or open the Notes app on your phone. Create three sections:

1. **Work Boundaries** – (e.g., "No responding to emails after 6 PM," "Decline additional shifts or schedule changes that don't benefit you")

2. **Family & Friends Boundaries** – (e.g., "Don't attend any event out of guilt," "Decline split bills unless agreed upon beforehand or take cash for your portion the bill")

3. **Personal Boundaries** – (e.g., "Protect mornings for self-care," "Honor scheduled rest without apology")

Keep this somewhere visible for the next 30 days as a visual reminder that *your time, energy, and peace are valuable*—and you don't need anyone else's permission to protect them.

CHAPTER 5

Declutter Your Life: A Detox for Your Mind, Space, and Soul

I'm sure we've all heard of a good old-fashioned detox. By definition, a detox is meant to rid the body of toxic or unhealthy substances. That definition sounds pretty similar to decluttering, which is to remove unnecessary items from a space. Now, what if we did both?

The stress we experience is not just in our heads. It's in our environment, our food, the people we surround ourselves with—it's EVERYWHERE. I see it the most in workplaces, my own and others'. And since I'm writing this book from my perspective, let me tell you what I've noticed.

In women, I see it in excessive weight gain. One day, someone looks one way, and the next time I see them, they've expanded, yet nothing in their life has changed—same job, same stress, same habits. A person who loves their life, feels at peace, and values themselves does not neglect their well-being. Someone who is fulfilled and genuinely at peace prioritizes their body and health—and no, I'm not saying they all count calories. But I am saying they think twice before picking up a second bag of chips, or they just skip the chips altogether.

A person excited about their work shows up with a smile, ready to tackle the day—not someone who drags their feet, searching for every reason to complain. A person who is confident prioritizes movement, whether it's hitting the gym, going for an outdoor walk, or taking the stairs when they could take the elevator. Someone who is happy and confident walks into work ready to spread joy instead of mumbling, "Ugh, the weekend wasn't long enough."

And honestly? If you only have two days off per week, I get why you don't take care of yourself. You don't even have the time to. How can you pour into others, when you are failing to pour into yourself.

The Noise in Your Life is Keeping You Stuck

If you're working 4-5 days a week, then spending your 2-3 days off trying to clean the house, meal plan, grocery shop, work out, spend time with family, cater to your spouse, care for the kids, and even consider a moment for yourself—you're stretched thin. You probably don't feel fulfilled or refreshed when it's time to head back to work. I've been there. I've done that. It sucks. And I will never do it again. Even if my family were in dire need of me working full-time, I'd find another way to contribute.

I refuse to run my precious time and life into the cement. I come first. You come first. So how can we start prioritizing you? What areas of your life bring you the most stress, and how can we start changing that narrative?

Activity: Get Rid of 10 Things That No Longer Serve You

This can be physical, mental, or social. If it no longer serves you, it's dead weight. Let it go.

Here's a list of 10 things I got rid of that no longer served me:

1. Toxic friends – If it's too much work and stress to maintain the friendship, YOU GOT TO GO.
2. Instagram followers/people I was following – If your lifestyle triggers me, YOU GOT TO GO.
3. Family members on Facebook – If I don't like you (and trust me, I LOVE people, but still), YOU GOT TO GO.
4. Clothes – If you're too small for these thighs and this ass, YOU GOT TO GO.
5. Shoes – If I haven't worn you in a year, YOU GOT TO GO.
6. Credit cards – If there's an annual fee, YOU GOT TO GO.
7. Toxic family members – If you disrespect me more than once, YOU GOT TO GO.
8. School books – I had books for taking the MCAT… but I'm never going to medical school. THEY HAD TO GO.
9. Anything non-holiday-related in my garage – YOU GOT TO GO.
10. Instagram – I went 9 months without that app because people forget it's JUST AN APP. IT HAD TO GO!
11.

Toxic Friendships: A Hard Lesson in Letting Go

Let me tell you something—I've had some questionable characters in my life. Some were just energy suckers I kept around out of pity, others were people I once proudly called "friends" who, in hindsight, were more of a liability than a light.

There was one in particular—a friend I once held close—who I eventually realized was a walking red flag. I'm talking about a full-time crisis, a drama magnet, a professional victim. Every interaction felt like I was doing unpaid emotional labor. And to my knowledge, there was no major trauma, just an endless storm of confusion and chaos. I almost included the full story of how I ended that friendship in this book, and some of the ladies on my editing team suggested If keep it, to aggressively edit it (it was bad lol, It was like a journal entry I needed to keep to myself lol). But after some thought, I asked myself: *What's the point of even telling that story?* They're not with me now. They're not headed where I'm going. So why should their far-from-a-legacy live on in these pages?

Let me be clear: They weren't the only one. Over time, I've learned that there are key characteristics in people that simply don't align with how I live and see the world. And that's okay. I now gravitate toward people who are like-minded, grounded, and vibrating high—and I distance myself from connections that feel forced or misaligned early on.

You know how in the dating world people say they have a "type"? I think we should normalize having a type in our friendships, too. You don't have to put people in boxes or exclude others unfairly, but you do have to honor your peace. Choose relationships that are high vibration. I'm talking about friends who leave a room and you still feel the joy they brought with them. You still feel full after they're gone. That's energy you want around.

But if someone leaves the room and you feel like less of yourself—like your body is finally relaxing after being on edge, your spirit is finding calm after chaos—then maybe that's not your person. If, on the other hand, they leave and you catch yourself smiling to yourself, laughing about something they said, or wanting to check on them to make sure they got home safe? Yeah, that might be your person.

Years of friendship do not equal a lifetime pass. I don't care if I've known you for 10 years—if the current version of you doesn't align with where I'm headed, you're not coming with me. That doesn't mean you can never join me later—life changes people. But I'm not dragging dead weight. I'm not sacrificing my peace for nostalgia. And once I stopped feeling guilty about that, my life started feeling a whole lot lighter.

Now, cutting off toxic friends and dead weight is one thing—but there's another kind of clutter that's just as dangerous: the noise of constant digital distractions. And let me tell you, when an acquaintance of mine pointed something out about my social media habits, it hit me just how powerful it is to step away and protect not just your space—but your *mind*, too...

Mini Action Step: Do a Friendship Energy Audit

Grab a sheet of paper and list the five people you spend the most time talking to or hanging around. Next to each name, write down how you typically feel *after* being around them—energized or drained, inspired or irritated, seen or silenced.

If even one of those names makes your stomach drop... you've got some reflecting to do. Don't ignore the signs. Your peace is too expensive to keep paying in discomfort.

MIA & Upgrading

An acquaintance pointed out that every time I go MIA from social media, I come back upgraded. Like, without fail. It's as if my disappearance signals that I'm in the lab cooking up something big, and when I finally reappear, there's some major life update waiting to be revealed.

And let me tell you—I LOVED this observation.

I have had an on-again, off-again relationship with social media since about 2023. Why? Because I believe real progress happens when you eliminate distractions. I get 24 hours in a day, and 8-9 of those hours are spent sleeping. That leaves me 14 hours per day to do something meaningful with my life. So why the hell would I waste excessive amounts of my time watching other people live out a 30-second, highly edited, clickbait version of their reality?

I want to live mine.

I remember hearing that Lamborghini doesn't make TV commercials because their ideal buyers aren't sitting at home watching TV. And baaaaybeeeeee, that statement had me feeling a tightness in my chest. Like, wait… do rich people not even have couches? Do they prefer sitting damn near on the floor like they would in that short-ass car?Or am I just a lazy bum by their standards?! Lmao.

Anyway, back to my point—I take frequent digital detoxes from Instagram and Facebook to reclaim my time and actually do something with it.

I remember going nine months without posting on IG, and people really thought I had some big baby announcement on the way. Meanwhile, in reality? My husband and I were living in Los Angeles, in an overpriced 450-square-foot studio, so he could pursue his music dreams, while I was:

- Taking the hardest board exam in my field (and passing it).
- Completing a mental toughness challenge that had me questioning my own sanity.
- Relocating across the country to L.A. for most of 2024 with no concrete plan, just faith and vibes.
- Paying off cars, student loans, and all those insane credit cards we once thought were a blessing but turned out to be a financial chokehold.
- Celebrating our fifth year of marriage with a dream vacation that felt too good to be real.

I was MIA, but I wasn't sitting around doing nothing. I was building. And even though I wasn't creating life in my belly, I was creating life around me—

- ✓ Making myself more valuable in my career.
- ✓ Supporting my husband as he chased his dream.
- ✓ Learning real financial literacy and breaking generational cycles.
- ✓ Losing 25+ pounds through healthy eating and movement.
- ✓ Exploring scenic hikes and actually appreciating nature (who knew that was a thing?).
- ✓ Attending personal and professional development conferences.

When I finally came back from MIA mode, I had:

- A schedule where I now need to work about 85 days per year (yes, 85).
- A second book in progress (because why stop at one?).
- A life that genuinely excites me, with a path so fulfilling that the day people start paying me to do what I love will feel like a "pinch me" moment—where a dream finally made it off my pillow and into reality.

So, what's the takeaway? People see you. Even when you think no one is watching, they are. And what you show people will always be more powerful than what you tell them. Because at the end of the day, actions speak.

The truth? You only NEED:

1. God
2. Food
3. Water
4. Shelter
5. Community

Everything else? Extracurricular.

Mini Action Step: Take a 72-Hour MIA Challenge

Log off all social media for the next 72 hours. No scrolling, no posting, no peeking. Instead, use that time to do something for your future self. Revisit a goal you put on the back burner. Read a book that's been collecting dust. Take a walk without your phone. Journal about what you want to "come back upgraded" with. Then, when (and if) you return online, let your glow speak louder than a post ever could.

Minimalism vs. Maximalism: Finding Balance in Simplicity

Now, I'm not saying I've gotten rid of everything—I'm not a minimalist, but I'm far from a maximalist. This might be the first time you've even seen either of those terms. A minimalist wants simplicity. A maximalist wants excess.

But don't let the word "simplicity" fool you—I still want a luxurious life. I like nice things, but I also like peace more. I'm not cheap, but I'm also not loose and reckless with money.

I don't feel the need to buy new clothes for every vacation. I don't need to keep up with the latest gadgets. I love my automatic, paid-off car and don't see the need to replace it just for seat warmers and push-to-start. I'd rather cook at home most nights, and when I do go out, I tip waiters so high that they ask if we need change—or I leave a tip so big that we skate out before they can say thank you.

Now that I've got a few extra years of maturity under my belt since I started really vacationing about six years ago, I realize how ridiculous it is to buy new clothes for every trip. Maybe one or two new outfits, sure—but I used to buy an entire vacation wardrobe down to the undies. Like, who am I doing this for? These people don't know me. They've never seen the inside of my closet. They don't know if my clothes are new, used, from Goodwill, hand-me-downs, or straight out of 2015. So why was I wasting money trying to impress strangers?

Wear your old clothes, at least some of them.

The amount of money you spend on new vacation outfits every year could probably cover another trip—or at the very least, give you a few extra days off work to tackle that never-ending to-do list. Think twice before you start buying trendy items or shopping just to keep up appearances. Nobody cares. Literally, nobody.

I can't recall a single time I've paid attention to whether someone's vacation wardrobe was new, stylish, or even high-quality. Hell, when I'm a couple drinks in, I'll compliment a pair of shoes with holes in them just because I'm feeling good and I believe everything has some beauty to it—even raggedy shoes.

So, this is my message to you: Stop buying things you can't afford. Stop trying to impress people who aren't even paying attention. And stop holding onto things you have no intention of using anytime soon (like, in the next 90 days).

Holding Onto Stuff Won't Fix Your Life

Let's talk about greed. A lot of people hold onto so much shii simply because they don't know how to let go. They want to keep all their stuff, accumulate other people's stuff, and still buy more stuff. Their homes are overflowing, their closets look like a department store clearance rack, and now they need to hire a professional organizer because their cleaning skills were subpar to begin with—and instead of getting it together, they just kept piling more chaos on top of it.

I'm the daughter of a professional organizer. I've been inside a lot of homes, helped my mom draft invoices estimating how long it would take to declutter a space—whether it was a studio apartment or a suburban mansion. I've seen hundreds, maybe even thousands of photos. And let me tell you, people have **a lot** of stuff.

I once read a book—I wish I could remember the name—but it explained how homes started getting bigger in the 19th century. Houses expanded, garages were added, cars grew larger, and now we have more bathrooms than people in the home. So what did folks do with all that extra space? They filled it. Somewhere along the way, people equated square footage with the need for more *stuff.*

Your environment is cluttered because your mind is cluttered. You hate the mess, your spouse hates the mess, but the real issue? You never learned how to let go. And the worst part? Much of this stock-piling comes from fear.

The way people stock-pile things today is on a whole new level. COVID, winter storms, the media—they've all conditioned us to believe that at any moment, we're going to run out of something essential and be left to fend for ourselves in some kind of apocalyptic wasteland. So what do people do? They panic-buy nonsense.

Like when people hear a winter storm is coming—and suddenly they rush to the store and buy 100 rolls of toilet paper, as if the snow is going to magically increase their bowel movements. I mean, why? What about the temperature drop outside makes you think your digestive system is about to start working overtime? It makes no sense.

And don't even get me started on the "just in case" mentality. Christians are literally taught in the Bible not to live in fear:

"Fear not, for I am with you; be not dismayed, for I am your God; I will strengthen you, I will help you, I will uphold you with my righteous right hand." – Isaiah 41:10

But what do most people do? Give in to the same fear traps as everyone else and start stockpiling like the world is ending tomorrow. And let's talk about this credit card fear-mongering. You always have to have a credit card "just in case of an emergency", right? That's what they tell you. But you know what else the Bible says?

"The rich rule over the poor, and the borrower is slave to the lender."
– Proverbs 22:7

Let me remind you—the first credit card was introduced in the 1950s. And guess what? Emergencies existed before credit cards. People still managed to survive, eat, pay rent, and move on with life—without owing 20% interest on it. If credit cards were really for emergencies, the banks wouldn't be charging you a ridiculous amount of interest if you couldn't afford to pay back your emergency within 30 days.

Let me put you on game. You can become your own credit card if you just start an emergency fund. Start with $1,000 and have it readily available. Put it in a high-yield savings account that earns 3-4% interest while it just sits there. And BOOM—you now have a financial safety net that isn't being controlled by a bank that wants to make money off your emergencies.

Now, let's talk about all those damn papers you're holding onto. Receipts. Junk mail. Letters. Bank statements from 2009. WHY? Digitize that shii and move on. I simply scan my documents using my overpriced iPhone and store them in the cloud with an easy-to-search name—so in the rare event that I actually need a receipt from 13 years ago, I can find it in two seconds.

This is a nice balance between the whole "what if I need it" paranoia and not wanting to drown in paper clutter. And if you're worried about hackers? Encrypt the file with a password and move on, Linda.

Declutter Your Life: Because Less is More

Your cluttered space, your overwhelming schedule, and your toxic relationships aren't just annoying inconveniences—they are holding you back. Less is most certainly more.

Now, grab a pen and write this down:

"Less noise, more peace." - Theresa Jenkins

So what are you holding onto that's keeping you from the life you deserve?

CHAPTER 6

Let's Build a life you don't need a vacation from!

Stop Living for the Weekend and Start Living for Life

If you have been living for the weekend, you are NOT living. Baby, the weekend is such a weak reward for surviving one out of 52 weeks. The weekend is eight days per month at best. And remember when I told you I get 20 days off per month? Yeah, I need more than just a weekend to live this good life and bring all these grand ideas in my head to reality. The weekend is like a snack or an appetizer before the main course. Living for the weekend is like doing 90% of the work and then getting a 10% accomplishment badge—and I don't know about you, but that sounds unfulfilling to me.

Let's break it down. If you work Monday through Friday, Saturday is your only real day of freedom, and by Sunday, you're already prepping for the next business week. You don't even fully enjoy it because the looming reality of Monday starts creeping in. Now, let me hit you with some real metrics because I don't want you thinking I'm just talking.

The Numbers That Should Wake You Up

Do you realize that working five days per week means you're working 240 days per year? And yeah, I know, you get some PTO and sick time, but let's be real—what's that? 20 days max? That means you're still working about 70% of the year just to have 30% left to enjoy your life.

Eww. What the fireball? That is NOT it, babes.

You couldn't pay me $100/hour to work that many days per year, and I knnooooow most people—especially employees—are not making anywhere close to that. And if you're one of those people stuck in the "retirement" mindset, then guess what? You're working 70% of the year for 70% of your life. The average life expectancy is 77.5 years. If you start working at 16 and don't retire until 65, that means you just spent the majority of your life working. And then what? I'm not going to finish that sentence.

What have you worked for?
What have you actually lived for?

Let's chalk this shii up and talk about how to get you living a life you don't need a vacation from.

How to Start Working Less and Living More

In Chapter 3, we talked about financial freedom and creating a budget. Now, it's time to analyze that budget and figure out what we can cut or decrease so you can start reclaiming your time. I want you to consider three options:

1. **Aggressive Approach** – Reduce your monthly expenses by **30%**.
    - Multiply your total monthly expenses by **0.30**, and that's your minimum target for expense reduction.

2. **Moderate Approach** – Reduce your monthly expenses by **15%**.
    - Multiply your total monthly expenses by **0.15**, and that's your minimum target for expense reduction.

3. **Passive Approach** – Reduce your monthly expenses by **10%**.
    - Multiply your total monthly expenses by **0.10**, and that's your minimum target for expense reduction.

For example, if your monthly expenses are $3,000:

Using my aggressive model, you would cut $900/month.
Using my moderate model, you would cut $450/month.
Using my passive model, you would cut $300/month.

Practical Ways to Cut Expenses Without Being Miserable

- Subscriptions: Cancel anything you forgot existed or barely use. You don't need every streaming service—pick 1-2 favorites and let the rest go. Trust me, your wallet won't miss them.
- Groceries: If food keeps rotting in your fridge, that's literally money in the trash. Start planning meals around what you already have before buying more. And let's talk about overspending—if you're dropping more than $50-$75 per person per week, it's too much. I lived in Los Angeles, California and fed two people on $500/month—high-protein diet, three meals a day, snacks and protein shakes. My family friend feeds a family of FIVE (including teenagers) on $400/month. So yeah, cut that grocery bill.

- Takeout: Reduce it by one time per week and put that money toward something more exciting than a lukewarm burger.
- Impulse Shopping: Target doesn't need any more of your money just because you "ran in for one thing". Stick to your list. Seriously.
- Ask yourself before buying: Do I actually need this, or did marketing just catch me in a weak moment? Be honest.

Cut the fluff, keep the fun, and free up your cash for things that actually matter.

Now Let's Talk About Your Work Hours

I don't know how much you make per hour, but let's say you're making $20/hour. How many hours would you have to work to make $900, $450, and $300?

First, let's define gross income—that's the amount you "earn" before taxes and deductions. I use the word gross here because it's the gross lie your employer tells you when they hire you, knowing damn well you'll never see the full amount. Haha. Net income, like a fish net, is what's actually left over after everyone takes their cut from your paycheck.

Now, let's get into the math. If you make $20/hour working 40 hours per week:

- Reducing your expenses by $900, you can work 45 hours less per month.
- Reducing your expenses by $450, you can work 22 hours less per month.

- Reducing your expenses by $300, you can work 15 hours less per month.

Now, if you're making $40/hour working part-time at 20 hours per week—let's discuss your reduction in work hours. Someone earning $40/hour could:

- Passive model ($300 reduction) = **8 fewer hours** per month
- Moderate model ($450 reduction) = **12 fewer hours** per month
- Aggressive model ($900 reduction) = **24 fewer hours** per month

By strategically cutting expenses, you are literally buying back your time. And what's better than having more time for yourself, your family, your passions, and even a little time to do absolutely nothing without guilt?

An alternative approach to working less—while still using the expense reduction model—is to reallocate the money you free up in a way that actually benefits your life. Instead of just cutting costs to work less, you can use that extra money strategically to create more freedom and stability for yourself.

You could:

- Build a fully funded emergency fund of 4-6 months of expenses.
- Pay down your consumer debt to lower your overall monthly expenses long-term.
- Save for your kids' college or fund your or your spouse's education if that's a goal.
- Invest in a business that can eventually bring in passive income.
- Save for a family vacation so you can enjoy life more often, not just in retirement.

- Put more money into retirement investments and speed up your financial independence.
- Donate to a charity or cause that aligns with your values.
- Stop living paycheck to paycheck, since you've freed up $900 extra per month to do whatever you want with.
- Make updates to your home, whether that's remodeling, decorating, or just upgrading things for comfort.
- Treat yourself to a spa day—because self-care is a necessity, not a luxury. (For reference, my favorite spa day costs $250 and includes a facial, massage, foot treatment, wine, and snacks. Worth every penny!)

There's so much you can do with your money once you free up some of it—but the most important thing? You now have the choice.

And before we wrap up, I need you to write this down:

Time is the only currency you can never get back. Use it wisely. The money? That will always be there to be made later.

Building a Life You Don't Need to Escape From

Let me tell you something—I am not about that life of working myself into the ground just to "deserve" a vacation. No, ma'am. I am crafting a life I don't need to escape from. That means being intentional with my time, my money, and my energy. It means shifting my focus from earning to living.

The old-school model of work until you retire is outdated and exhausting. I mean, do you really want to spend 70% of your year working, only to reach the age of 65, finally have time, and then…

what? Hope that your body, mind, and spirit are still in good enough shape to actually enjoy the life you spent decades waiting for?

Nope. Not me. And hopefully, not you either.

So, the next step? Decide what kind of life you want to live and pick a path that gets you there faster. Do you want to aggressively restructure your life, cut unnecessary spending, and reclaim as much time as possible? Or do you prefer a moderate approach, where you still enjoy some of your comforts but start trimming the fat? Maybe you're more of a passive adjuster, easing into this lifestyle one step at a time. Either way, you're making progress.

One thing is certain—you cannot keep living for the weekend and expect to feel fulfilled. That's not a life, that's a countdown clock. A two-day appetizer to a five-day meal of exhaustion. The goal isn't to work just so you can get two small bites of freedom. The goal is to build a life where freedom isn't something you have to wait for—it's something you live every day.

Alright, less thinking and more doing. Here's what I want you to do right now:

Action Step: Buy Back Your Time

1. Choose your expense reduction plan.
Are you going aggressive (30%), moderate (15%), or passive (10%)? Pick one that matches your current energy and goals.

2. Write down 3 quick wins.
What are three things you can reduce or cut this month—without

feeling deprived? Think:

- Subscriptions you forgot you had.
- Takeout that's become a habit.
- Grocery bills that could be trimmed with better planning

Start there. Simple cuts add up fast.

3. Calculate how much time you're buying back.
Take the dollar amount you're saving (from step 1), and divide that number by your current hourly wage.
Example: If you're going to cut expenses by $450/month and you make $20/hour, that's 22.5 hours you no longer have to work.
This step will show you how many hours of your life you're reclaiming each month just by cutting a few expenses.

4. Decide what you'll do with your reclaimed time.
Don't leave this part blank. Time is like money—if you don't tell it where to go, it disappears.
Will you rest? Create? Read? Launch your side hustle? Reconnect with people you love? Write it down. Intention turns free time into fulfilled time.

5. Commit to the shift—today.
Don't just nod and move on. Actually take one action right now.

- Cancel a subscription
- Skip an unnecessary purchase
- Plan how you will ask your management or leadership team about working fewer hours.

Small steps move mountains when done consistently. Choose one and go.

Let me remind you: time is the only currency you can never get back. You don't get a refund on wasted years, and you can't buy back the time you spent grinding for money that's already gone.

So, what's it going to be? More hours worked—or more life lived? Your move.

CHAPTER 7

How Has Cancel Culture Not Canceled Monday?

Cancel culture wastes no time shutting down anything it deems unjust or unpopular—so why the hell hasn't it canceled Monday yet?

Let's be real: Monday is the most common day for people to call in sick. Monday is also the least favorite day of the week. If any of those facts surprise you, go ahead and close this book—I'll have my assistant issue you a refund. Just kidding. I don't have an assistant, and there are no refunds. I'm currently sitting on a couch I bought from Rooms To Go, wrapped in a blanket gifted to me at my wedding. Moving on. Monday sucks.

Monday shows up uninvited, unannounced, and unwanted—like an ex who still "checks in" every few months. One minute you're winding down your Sunday, maybe going to church, maybe meal prepping like a responsible adult, and then BOOM—Monday slaps the relaxation right off your face. Another week of the same chaotic work shenanigans that play on repeat 52 weeks a year.

And the only Mondays I've ever enjoyed? The ones where I didn't have to spend them around other people who also hate Mondays.

Now, granted, I officially retired from working Mondays as of March 31st (and no, I didn't get a cookie party—shocker). But that's okay. I'll be there on Wednesday, and I'm sure my coworkers still won't celebrate my milestone.

For most people, Monday is the start of the workweek—and the start of their misery. After a weekend of sleeping in, sipping mimosas, and briefly forgetting about their responsibilities, Monday drags them right back into reality. The noisy alarm goes off, emails about bills flood their inbox, their kid's school bus blocks both lanes of traffic, and the neighbor's Yorkie with the ridiculous bow starts barking at absolutely nothing.

Then, they finally get to work—only to be greeted by a building full of equally miserable people. I dare you to count how many times someone mutters the word "coffee" before noon. Better yet, count how many people are clutching a coffee like it's a life-saving IV drip.

All that extra sleep they supposedly "caught up on" over the weekend, and yet, here they are—still exhausted, still over it, still not ready for Monday's corporate circus. I've said this out loud before, and this will be the first time I write it down: ***People should be getting paid shift differential just for working on Mondays.*** Because let's be honest—nobody is voluntarily signing up for that nonsense.

What Makes Monday the Worst? Well, Tuesday and Wednesday pretty much feel the same—just an extension of the weekly drag. But Thursday? Thursday is "Friday Eve." By then, you're close enough to the weekend that you can taste it.

Friday, on the other hand, is everybody's favorite coworker. Even the most caffeine-dependent among us need less coffee to survive a Friday than to survive a Monday. I once watched a guy drink six or seven coffees on a Monday. I exaggerate a lot—but I'm not exaggerating now.

Saturday? Best day of the week, hands down. Sunday? Chill… until the Sunday Scaries roll in around noon and start haunting you like a ghost of uncompleted tasks past. Which brings me back to my point—Mondays are the worst.

The Game Plan: Cancel Mondays from Your Schedule

As an author, my job is to take you from Point A: stressed as hell to Point B: not stressed—or at least significantly less stressed.

So here's my advice:
If you have the power to rearrange your work schedule, let Monday be the first day you eliminate.

Spending Mondays at home—whether alone or with family—is 100x better than dealing with the collective agony of the workforce. If you must leave the house, stick to the gym between 11 AM and 2 PM, when the Monday crowd is either at work or still drowning themselves in caffeine. Otherwise? Avoid public spaces.

On Monday's traffic is a nightmare. Stores are full of overachievers who think Monday is the best day to be productive because they refuse to run errands on weekends. Everyone you encounter is annoyed—because, well, it's Monday.

Now, let me share a little insight from someone who has way too much free time to analyze traffic patterns and store busyness. The best day to run errands?

TUESDAY.

When I go to Costco on a Tuesday, I don't have to say "excuse me" to anyone. I can eat all the free samples if I want to. (I don't—because I eat before I grocery shop, so I don't impulse-buy nonsense.) I park right by the entrance—prime real estate. I get gas with no wait. There's zero traffic getting there—or getting home.

So, my advice? Break up with Mondays. Stay home. Do all the things you love from home. Then, when you're ready to re-enter the world, do it on your own damn terms.

Monday can officially see itself out.

Action Step: The Monday Exit Plan

Ask yourself: *What would your life look like if Mondays weren't a thing?*

- If you're employed, explore whether your schedule can be adjusted. Can you negotiate a four-day workweek? Shift your hours to start on Tuesday? Take one Monday off next month and see how your mood shifts.
- If you're self-employed, commit to treating Monday as your **personal CEO day**—no meetings, no errands. Just vision work, planning, and rest.
- No matter your job, choose one obligation you *typically* do on a Monday—and move it to another day.

This is how you reclaim control: not all at once, but one intentional shift at a time.

CHAPTER 8

The Freedom Formula: Owning your time like a BOSS

Priorities. That's the first word I want you to take in. Some people say control is an illusion, but I believe control is a skill—and like any skill, you can get better at it.

Sure, you can't dictate every second of your day. Life happens. But you can control certain narratives. You control whether or not you eat, what temperature your house is set to (assuming you pay the bills), and whether you eat your calories or drink them—by the way, drinking your calories is one of the worst culprits of weight gain. Drink. More. Water.

You control whether you pay for daycare or if you and your partner strategically adjust work schedules to have one of you home with the kids. You control more than you think—you just may not be good at managing your free time.

So how do you structure your off days to breathe easier and feel more free?

The Rule of Three Priorities

From now on, we're going to simplify your to-do list. You get three priorities per day—no more, no less. That doesn't mean you can't do other things, but it does mean you won't beat yourself up over what didn't get done. This method forces you to prioritize what truly matters.

Here's how I break it down:

1. One priority for me (self-care, health, enjoyment).
2. One priority for my future/business (something that moves me forward).
3. One priority is to enhance my home (because a peaceful home = a peaceful mind).

Examples of Priorities for Me

- A 45-minute workout.
- An outdoor walk.
- At-home pedicure or full self-care day.
- A 1-hour massage.
- Watching a show guilt-free.
- Reading a personal development book and journaling.

Examples of Priorities for My Future/Business

- Goal setting or revisiting my vision board.
- Writing and editing a chapter for my book.
- Brainstorming and recording a YouTube video.
- Engaging in learning (course, seminar, etc.).

Examples of Priorities for My Home

- Planning the grocery list and meal plan (this takes time—so it gets its own day).
- Grocery shopping (I hit 3 stores biweekly—this is an event).
- Doing all the laundry.
- Cleaning the house top to bottom.
- Vacuuming, mopping, swapping out scent plug-ins.
- Cooking a meal.
- Prepping overnight oats (because future me will thank me).

A Sample Week in My Life

As someone who is usually home five days per week, here's how I structure my days:

Monday: Do my hair (3+ hour process), plan & record a YouTube video, cook one meal.
Tuesday: Work. That's it. Maybe enjoy a glass of wine with my husband.
Wednesday: Work. Come home and rot on the couch guilt-free.
Thursday: Extended outdoor walk with my dog, plan & record a YouTube video, cook one meal.
Saturday: Read & journal, write a book chapter, meal plan/grocery list.
Sunday: Try Pilates, write a book chapter, grocery shopping event.

Notice anything? No two days look the same. On workdays, I don't overcommit myself. I already leave the house for 9-12 hours, so if I have energy when I get home, great—but if I don't, so what? The dishes will still be there in the morning. Do what feels right, not what will stress you out.

The Power Hour: A Game-Changer for Your Mornings

Every day—even on weekends—I naturally wake up by 6:30-7:00 AM. My husband wakes up around 9:00 AM, so I use that quiet time to pour into myself.

I start my day with:

- **Reading or journaling** (on the couch with natural light).
- **Opening all the blinds** (I like the sun waking up my space).
- **Letting my dog out and refilling her food/water** (so she leaves me alone).
- **Enjoying a protein shake** with a tablespoon of unsweetened peanut butter (a small joy).
- **Drinking at least 20 oz of water** before I do anything else.

Before anyone else needs me—before the emails, the calls, the husband, the dog, the world—I have already poured into myself.

I used to wake up at 5 AM after reading The 5 AM Club by Robin Sharma. At first, it was rough, but soon I noticed how differently I moved through my day. I had already centered myself before stepping into the chaos of work, traffic, and responsibility.

Meanwhile, others?

- They hit snooze until the last second.
- They rush into work half-awake.
- They skip breakfast or eat whatever is fast and sugary.
- They sit in traffic, already frustrated.
- They are running on fumes, stressed, and reactive all day.

They don't realize how much better they could feel with just one hour of stillness and preparation.

People would to say to me:

> "Wow, you're so calm."
> "I love how you handled that situation."
> "You eat so healthy!"
> "Wait... you already worked out today?"
> "You're going outside for a walk at lunch? But it's cold."
> "You get nine hours of sleep?! I barely get six."

I started realizing—most people don't even know how stuck they are. They think feeling rushed, stressed, exhausted, and behind is just how life works. They have no idea that a better version of themselves exists—they just have to make space for it.

The Power Hour Challenge

If you take one thing from this book, let it be this:

Create a Power Hour for yourself. Before the world gets loud. Before emails. Before responsibility. Just one hour every day for one week. Try it. If you love it, great—it'll change your life. If you hate it, go back to your old ways. But at least you'll know what it feels like to wake up in control of your day, instead of being thrown into it.

Once you master your **Power Hour**, consider a **Power Half-Hour** at Night:

- Wind down with a book (alone or with a partner).
- Share something powerful you read.

- Slow down before sleep—no scrolling, no noise.

If you have a partner, this is an intimate way to end the night together. You can read aloud to each other, share thoughts, or just exist in stillness together.

Final Thought: Slow Down, Smell the Damn Roses

If you don't intentionally create space for yourself, your peace, and your freedom, life will fill it with nonsense for you.

Control your time, or the world will control it for you.

Action Step: Build Your Freedom Week

Grab a pen, a piece of paper (or open your notes app—no judgment), and map out the next 7 days using the Rule of Three Priorities. For each day, list:

- **1 thing just for you** (self-care, fun, health)
- **1 thing for your future** (a goal, skill, or creative pursuit)
- **1 thing for your home** (organization, errands, or a chore)

Be realistic. If you work long shifts, your priority might be as simple as *resting intentionally*—and that counts. The goal here is freedom through structure, not perfection.

Set the tone for the week by scheduling one **Power Hour** in the morning—at least three times. Pick the days. Try it. See how it feels to wake up with intention, not obligation.

CHAPTER 9

Success-ing—Your new normal

I made up this word, and I stand by it. Successing. Because when you add -ing to the end of a word, it means something is actively happening—and that's exactly what success should be. Not a single event, not a finish line, but an ongoing process.

In this chapter, I want to talk about goals—big goals. The kind of goals so massive that you don't even want to tell anyone about them because you're afraid they'll laugh at you. The kind of goals that make people say, "Now, be realistic," and you have to resist the urge to roll your eyes.

It's easy to talk yourself out of setting big goals just because they don't seem practical or achievable right now. But let me ask you this—if you don't have something so extraordinary to work toward, what's keeping you motivated to strive for more in life?

Think about it. What's that one big goal that makes you feel slightly ridiculous for even writing it down?

Do you want to spend six months in Thailand?

Do you want to move to a Spanish-speaking country for a year so you can actually become fluent instead of just remembering the words for "bathroom" and "where is the library"?
Do you want to see penguins in their natural habitat instead of just on National Geographic?
Do you want to homeschool your kids around the world, giving them the best hands-on learning experiences they could ever get?

What do you want? What are your big, ridiculous, borderline-unbelievable goals?

Creating Your Own Opportunities

I don't know where you're reading this book, but I'm writing it from America, a country full of opportunities. But the real secret? You don't always have to wait for opportunities—you can create them.

Too often, people sit around waiting for things to fall into place instead of making things happen for themselves. But guess what? The most successful people you see out there? They didn't wait—they built, created, and took action.

Ever heard of someone who created a job for themselves that didn't even exist? That's not just something entrepreneurs do. Even in the workplace, you can propose a role, redefine your job, and carve out a space that fits your strengths and goals. It might not be common, but it's absolutely possible.

My Seven Big Goals

Since we're on this journey together, I'm going to be a little vulnerable here and share seven goals I've set for myself over the next five to seven years. These are the kind of goals that make me excited and slightly nervous, but hey—that's how I know they're big enough.

1. Sell 10,000 Copies of My First Self-Published Book

I wrote RVT in 10 Days: Your Path to Passing to teach study strategies to anyone willing to listen. 10,000 copies is the goal, and honestly, I'm well on my way.

2. Write a Nonfiction Chapter Book

It's March 2025 as I write this, and I set this goal in January. I'm already near the finish line on my nonfiction chapter book. So check this one off—almost!

3. Become the Highest Donor of a Nonprofit or Hospital

I want to make a significant impact, not just with my words but with my resources. This one is deeply personal to me, and when it happens, it will be one of my proudest accomplishments.

4. Live in Another Country for Six Months

I want to experience life outside the U.S., not as a tourist but as a temporary resident. New culture, new perspectives, and maybe even a new way of thinking about life.

5. Do a One-Year World Tour with My Husband (and Future Kids, If We Have Them by Then)

Travel is a passion, but I want to take it to the next level—a full year of exploring the world together. If we have kids by then, even better. What a way to raise a family!

6. Make My Fortune as a Public Speaker

I see myself traveling the country, speaking on ultrasound education, personal development, and life success. The day people start paying me to do what I love will be the day I know I've truly built something incredible.

7. Achieve Debt-Free Status—Including My Mortgage

My husband and I are already on track for this one, and let me tell you—financial freedom is the ultimate flex. No monthly debt payments, no financial stress, just pure options.

Action Step: Set Your 7 Big Goals

Alright, your turn.
Grab a piece of paper, open your notes app, or dust off that journal you only use for "important thoughts"—because this is one of those moments.

Write down **7 big, bold, and maybe slightly ridiculous goals** that you want to accomplish in the next **5 to 7 years**. These aren't your safe, polite goals. These are the "if everything went right, and I stopped playing small" goals.

Don't worry about how just yet. Just write them.
Want to live in Italy for six months? Put it down.
Want to quit your job and start a business? Add it.
Want to retire early? Say it.
Want to pay off your house, move to the beach, and only wear linen? GO FOR IT.

These goals are for your eyes first—so be honest, be daring, and remember: if your list doesn't scare you a little… it's probably not big enough.

The Doctorate Dream

This one deserves its own moment. I know I said seven, so consider this one a bonus goal! I've always loved education. I love learning, I love reading, I love teaching and I love writing.

When I was younger, I had dreams of becoming a doctor, but after a study abroad program in Spain showed me the reality of medical school, I quickly realized that wasn't quite for me.

But after years of experience, growth, and self-discovery, I now know that I still want to be a doctor—just not a medical doctor. I love the idea of holding a doctorate, achieving the highest level of education, and being called Dr. Theresa Jenkins.

And guess what? It's happening.

Story Time: Pre-Med to Sonography

Let's take it back to the beginning. I was on a full-ride scholarship that I secured in 8th grade. Yes, you read that right—8th grade! Huge shoutout to Montgomery County Ohio College Promise Scholarship—they changed the trajectory of my life, and for that, I'll always be grateful!

Fast forward to the summer between my sophomore and junior year of college. I found this incredible study abroad program that allowed U.S.

students to shadow medical doctors in Europe in exchange for teaching English. The moment I heard about it, I knew I had to make it happen. There was just one issue—the $7,000 price tag.

Now, my family wasn't in a financial position to fund an experience like this. But I wasn't about to let that stop me. I got creative. I started crowdfunding, wrote letters to every professional I could think of (yes, including my pediatrician—shoutout to them!), and even did a news interview at my house that aired on local television. It was all a hustle, but I made it happen.

At the time, I was pre-med, and this trip was meant to help me stand out for medical school applications. I knew my grades weren't top-tier—not because I wasn't smart, but because I didn't know how to study efficiently or take standardized tests well. So, I needed something extraordinary to set me apart.

Oh, and let's be real—I was also a Black woman in America, and at that time, I had let society convince me that medical schools wouldn't see me as their first choice. (Side note: That was a lie, and I've since unlearned that nonsense.)

The Unexpected Detour

During my study abroad program, I was able to choose specialties to shadow. One particular day, my assigned doctor couldn't make it to work, so I was redirected to the ultrasound department.

And that, my friends, is where everything changed.

I spent the day shadowing an ultrasound sonographer in Castilla-La Mancha, Spain, and I was fascinated. She had her own patients, worked closely with them one-on-one, and was actively involved in their care. Some of her patients were pregnant, and I remember seeing the joy on their faces as she walked them through what she was seeing on the screen.

At that moment, I realized something.

I had no idea there were medical careers that allowed you to have your own workflow, your own patients, and direct patient care—without being a medical doctor. My lack of knowledge about healthcare career options had tricked me into believing my only path was becoming a physician.

Before my study abroad experience, I had a friend back home who kept encouraging me to consider Sonography. But I was dead set on medical school and wasn't giving it the time of day. That all changed in Spain.

After finishing my rotations in dermatology, anesthesiology, general surgery, OB/GYN, and sonography, I immediately made an appointment with my academic counselor when I got back to the States. I changed my major from Pre-Medicine to Diagnostic Medical Sonography—and let me tell you, it was the best decision I ever made.

The Myth of "Too Late"

Now, let's talk about something important.

A lot of people—even my academic counselor—tried to convince me that changing my major as a junior was "too late" and "risky." But too late according to who?

People love projecting their own limitations onto you. They see things from their perspective—not yours. If I had listened to them, I wouldn't be where I am today.

Yes, I had to put in extra work to make it happen. I had to give up my summer break to take an advanced, accelerated Anatomy & Physiology course. I had to take an extra online course at a community college hours away. I had to enroll in an additional elective class over the summer to meet program requirements.

I was working nearly full-time work hours while juggling a full summer course load just to make sure I got into the Diagnostic Medical Sonography program by the fall.

Was it challenging? Yes. Did I let that stop me? Absolutely not.

If there's anything I want you to take away from this, it's this:
People will tell you what's "too hard," "too risky," or "too late"—but they don't have to live with the consequences of your decisions. YOU DO.

It is never "too late." It's not too late to go back to school. It's not too late to become a parent. It's not too late to rekindle that relationship that's been on your mind. It's not too late to tell your waiter you don't like your meal. It's not too late to put in that PTO request (it might actually get approved). It's not too late to do most things. Think big. Be bold!

Betting on Myself

Honestly, I've always been ambitious, and I've always trusted my own judgment—even when others doubted me. Nobody thought it was a great idea for me to go to college a few hours away from home. But I knew it was the best decision for me. Going "away" for college forced me to become independent. It made me think twice before running home whenever life got hard. It also taught me how to build a new community for myself.

I strategically chose a school far enough away to stop me from running home at every inconvenience, but close enough that I could visit when I truly needed to. Other people had limiting beliefs about what I could and should do—but I didn't listen to them. And let me just say, most of the people who encouraged me to stay closer hadn't gone away to college themselves. Their fear of the unknown worried them—but it empowered me.

Carving My Own Path

When I received my full-ride scholarship, the program came with a strict plan: two years at a community college, followed by two final years at a university. That plan? Yeah, it wasn't working for me. *LOL.* (Honestly, writing this book has me realizing—I've always been a little rebellious. Who knew?)

So, I rewrote my own path. I completed one year at community college (because let's be real, that first year is mostly general education anyway). Then, instead of staying for year two, I pushed my way into the university early. I worked directly with my scholarship program, explained my vision, and negotiated a new route to get where I wanted to go.

What's the lesson here?
You are *not* stuck. You do *not* have to follow a path just because someone else laid it out for you. If it's not working—*change it.* Make your own rules. Rewrite the plan.

I am where I am today because I:

1. Believed in myself.
2. Refused to let other people's doubts become my reality.
3. Took action, even when it was difficult.

I am grateful for my determination, for the people who helped me along the way, and for the faith I had in myself and in God. At the end of the day, success is not just about making the "right" choice the first time—it's about having the courage to adjust when you realize there's a better way.

So, if there's something in your life that isn't serving you, I challenge you to ask yourself: are you holding onto it because you want it, or because you're afraid to change directions? Because trust me—betting on yourself is always worth it.

Define Your Own Version of Success

Now, here's what I want you to think about:

1. What are YOUR big, unrealistic, slightly terrifying goals?
2. What opportunities can you create for yourself instead of waiting for them?

3. How do YOU define success?

Because success isn't a single destination—it's a lifelong journey.

So, let's get to successing.

About The Author

Theresa Jenkins is a woman who believes success is a feeling, not just a finish line. After redefining her own path—leaving behind the traditional 9-to-5 hustle—she now inspires others to pursue a life filled with freedom, alignment, and intention. She's a Sonographer, speaker, creative entrepreneur, and someone who knows what it's like to feel overwhelmed by life's demands. Through honest storytelling and actionable steps, Theresa shares how she transitioned from burnout to balance—and how you can too.

Made in the USA
Columbia, SC
08 June 2025

59047988R00057